Linda Niamath

LIE

ELEMENTARY PIANO SOLO

soda pop
and other delights

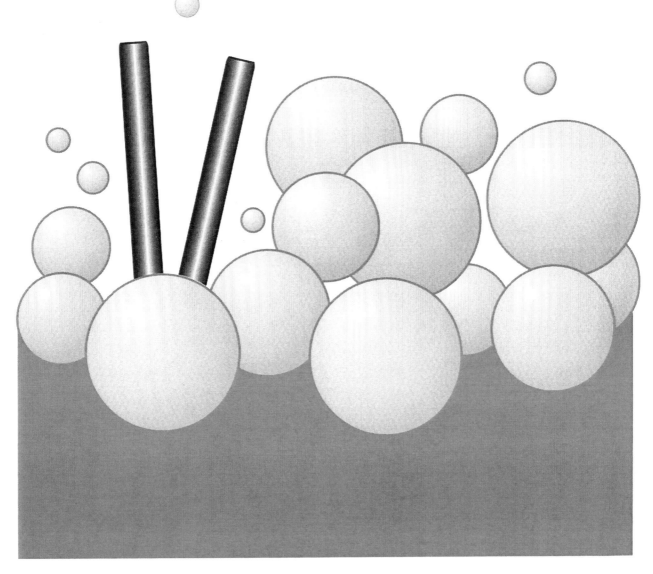

 Alfred Music
P.O. Box 10003
Van Nuys, CA 91410-0003
alfred.com

ISBN-10: 1-4706-4137-2
ISBN-13: 978-1-4706-4137-5

PREFACE

These short, descriptive pieces were written for the enjoyment of children in their early years of piano study. It is hoped that the pieces will aid young pianists in the development of their technical and interpretative skills. Captions and drawings have been provided to help stimulate students' imaginations.

Linda Niamath

Original cover design by Kathy Crowe

Illustrations by Cheryl and Wendy Niamath

Contents

Can you imagine that you are gently stroking a sleepy little kitten ?

Sleepy Little Kitten

Linda Niamath

Bubbles, bubbles, bubbles, bubbles,

Up they go to the top of your pop !

Soda Pop

Linda Niamath

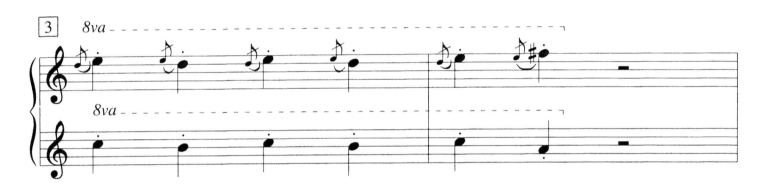

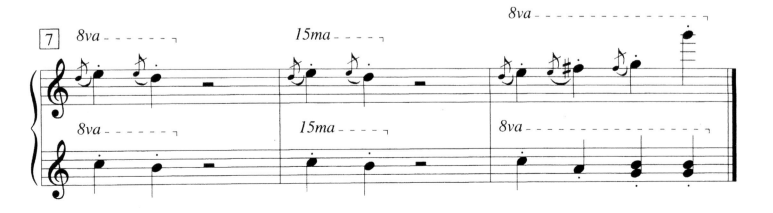

Here they come, Big Teddy showing
Little Teddy how to waltz.

Big Teddy, Little Teddy

Moderately, with warmth ♩ = 112

Linda Niamath

***You are smoothly gliding over the sparkling ice,
and you'll finish with an exciting spin.***

Skating

Linda Niamath

accelerando e crescendo al Fine

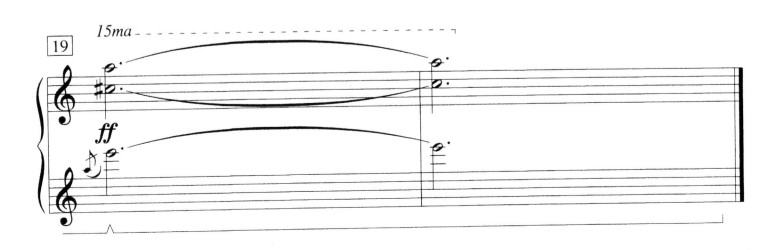

Where are you hiding —

upstairs or downstairs ?

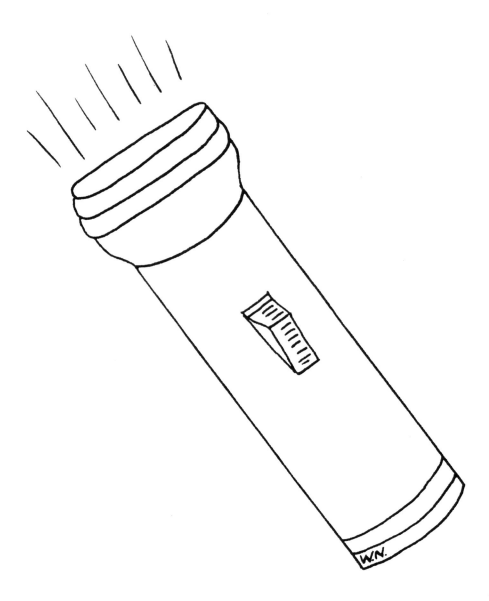

Hide and Seek

Linda Niamath

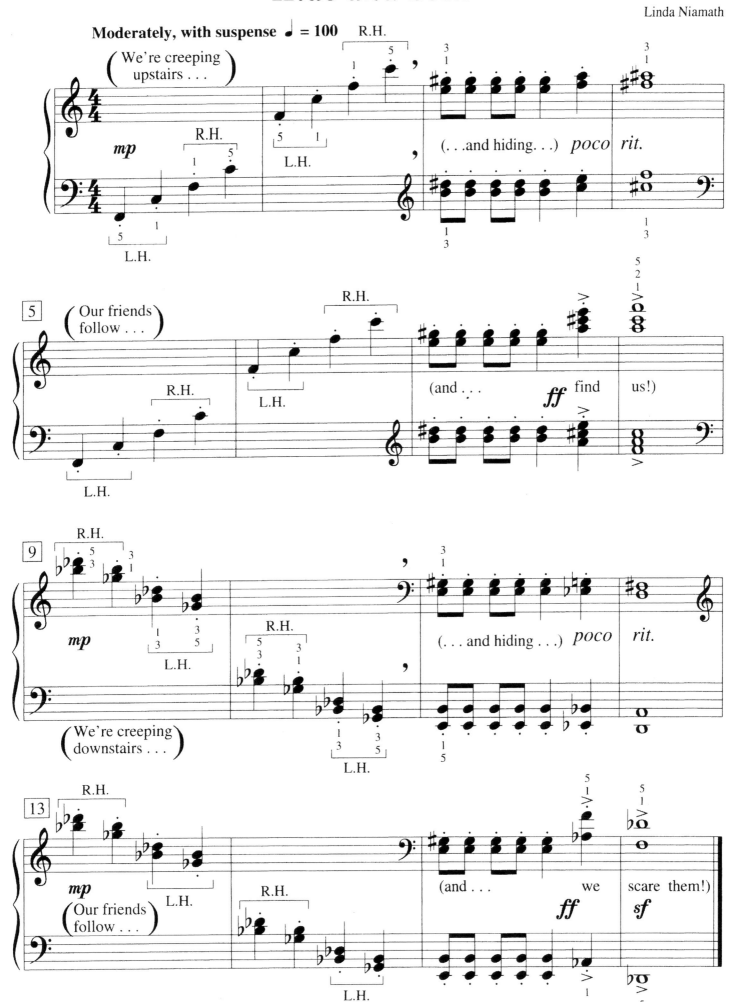

Princess — what has made you

feel so sad and lonely ?

The Lonely Princess

Linda Niamath

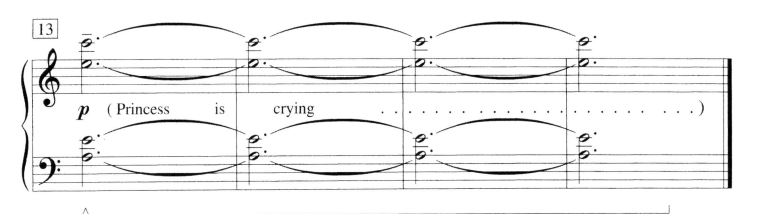

What tricks could this

little puppy be up to ?

Playful Puppy

Quickly and happily ♩ = 184

Linda Niamath

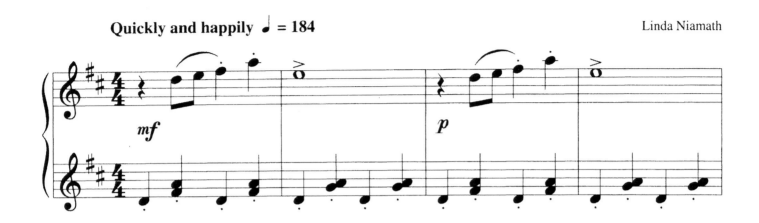

tail wagging

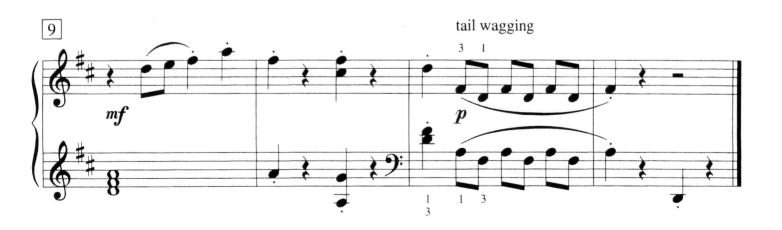

Watch out !

The Terrible Trolls are coming !

March of the Terrible Trolls

Linda Niamath

Happily swinging from branch to branch,

these little monkeys have lots of mischief in mind.

Monkey Mischief

Linda Niamath

Hurrah ! Hurrah !

It's the last day of school !

Holidays Are Here!

Linda Niamath

L.H.

NOTES FOR TEACHERS

Considerations for each piece

1. **Sleepy Little Kitten**

    phrasing
    syncopated pedalling

2. **Soda Pop**

    grace notes

3. **Big Teddy, Little Teddy**

    singing melody
    dotted rhythm
    imitation

4. **Skating**

    broken triads
    full keyboard span
    syncopated pedalling
    accelerando

5. **Hide and Seek**

    staccato
    contrasting dynamics
    shifting tonality

6. **The Lonely Princess**

    expressive melody
    ostinato accompaniment
    finger independence

7. **Playful Puppy**

    staccato
    contrasting dynamics

8. **March of the Terrible Trolls**

    triplets
    five-finger patterns
    left-hand fluency

9. **Monkey Mischief**

    two-note slurs
    five-note clusters

10. **Holidays are Here !**

    trills
    tonal shading
    syncopation
    glissando